AF544883

THE SILENT AFTERMATH OF SPACE

Published by Damiani editore
via Zanardi 376
40131 Bologna, Italy
t. +39 051 6350805 f. +39 051 6347188
info@damianieditore.it / www.damianieditore.it

ISBN 978-88-6208-112-2

THE SILENT AFTERMATH OF SPACE

PHOTOGRAPHS CALEB CAIN MARCUS
FOREWORD ROBERT FRANK

DAMIANI

FOREWORD

There is silence in the Bronx and Brooklyn.

Caleb, photographer, walks these streets photographing the light of night.

His view shows a quiet resignation and jubilation for being an artist and alone.

Have you ever heard the word Alptraum — maybe it is the German idea of Aftermath of Space.

WHO KNOWS?

Robert Frank 2009

The ringing
is the silence within us.

LONG ISLAND RAILROAD

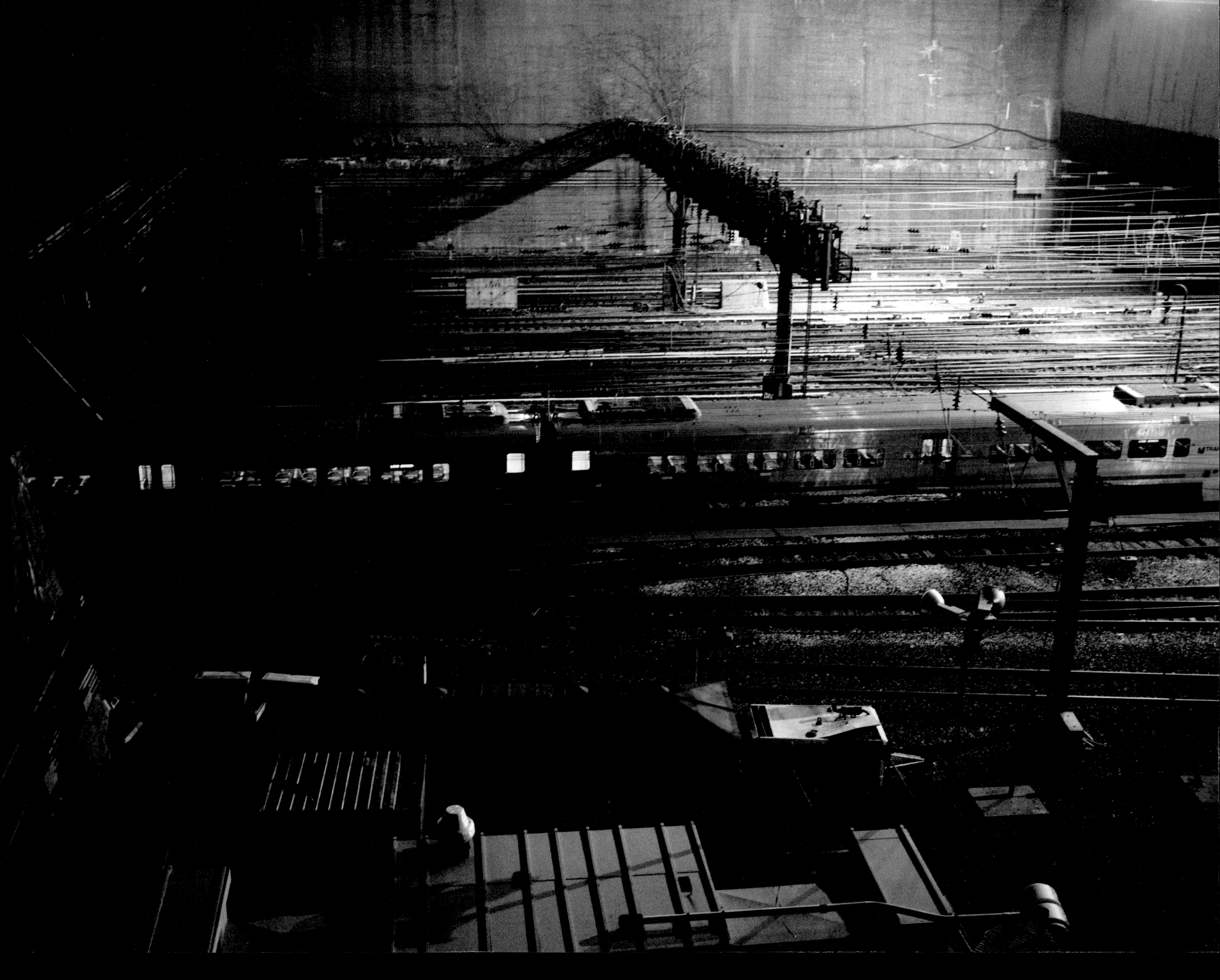

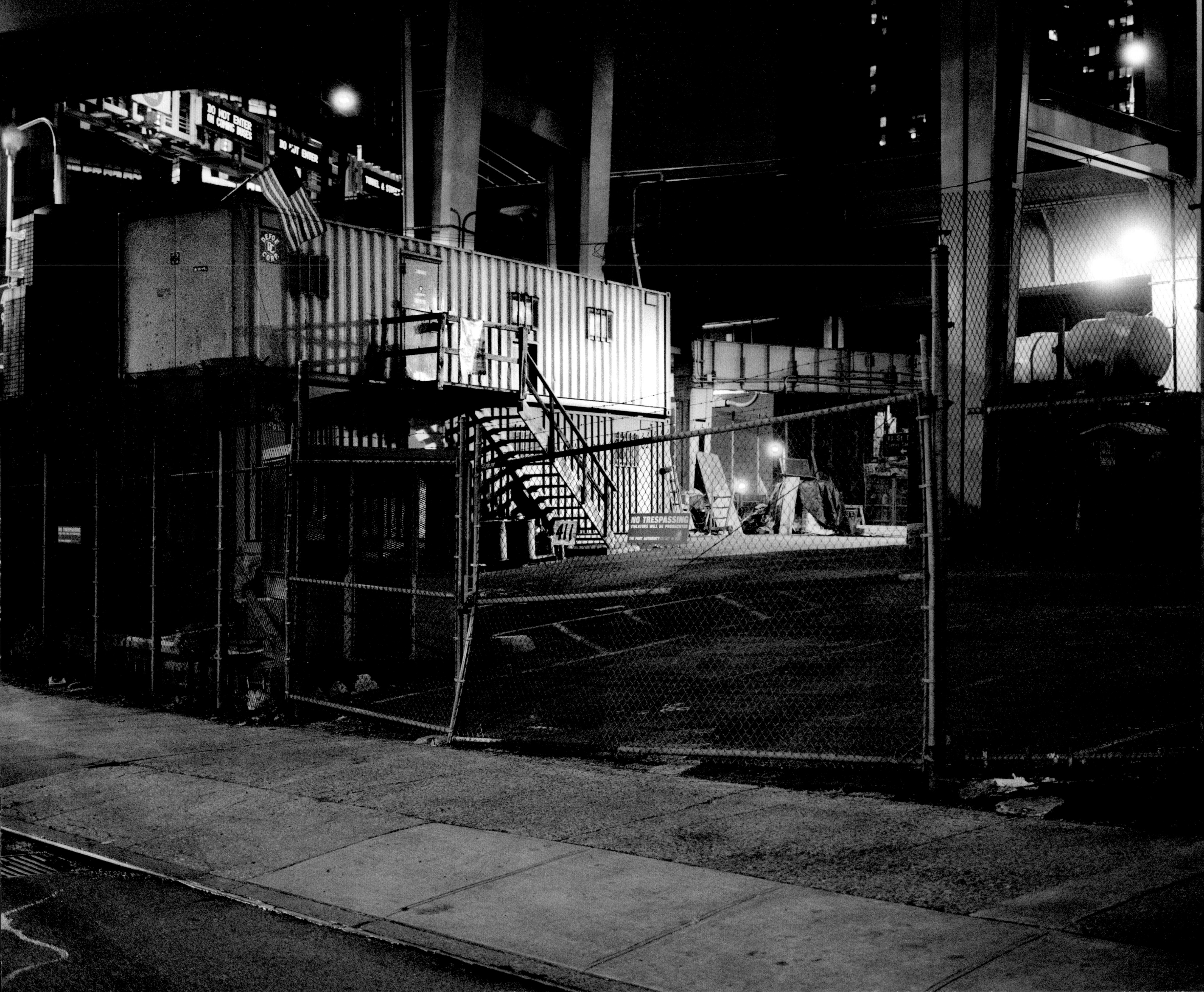
DO NOT ENTER
ON COMING BUSES
DO NOT ENTER
DEFOE
NO TRESPASSING
VIOLATORS WILL BE PROSECUTED
THE PORT AUTHORITY

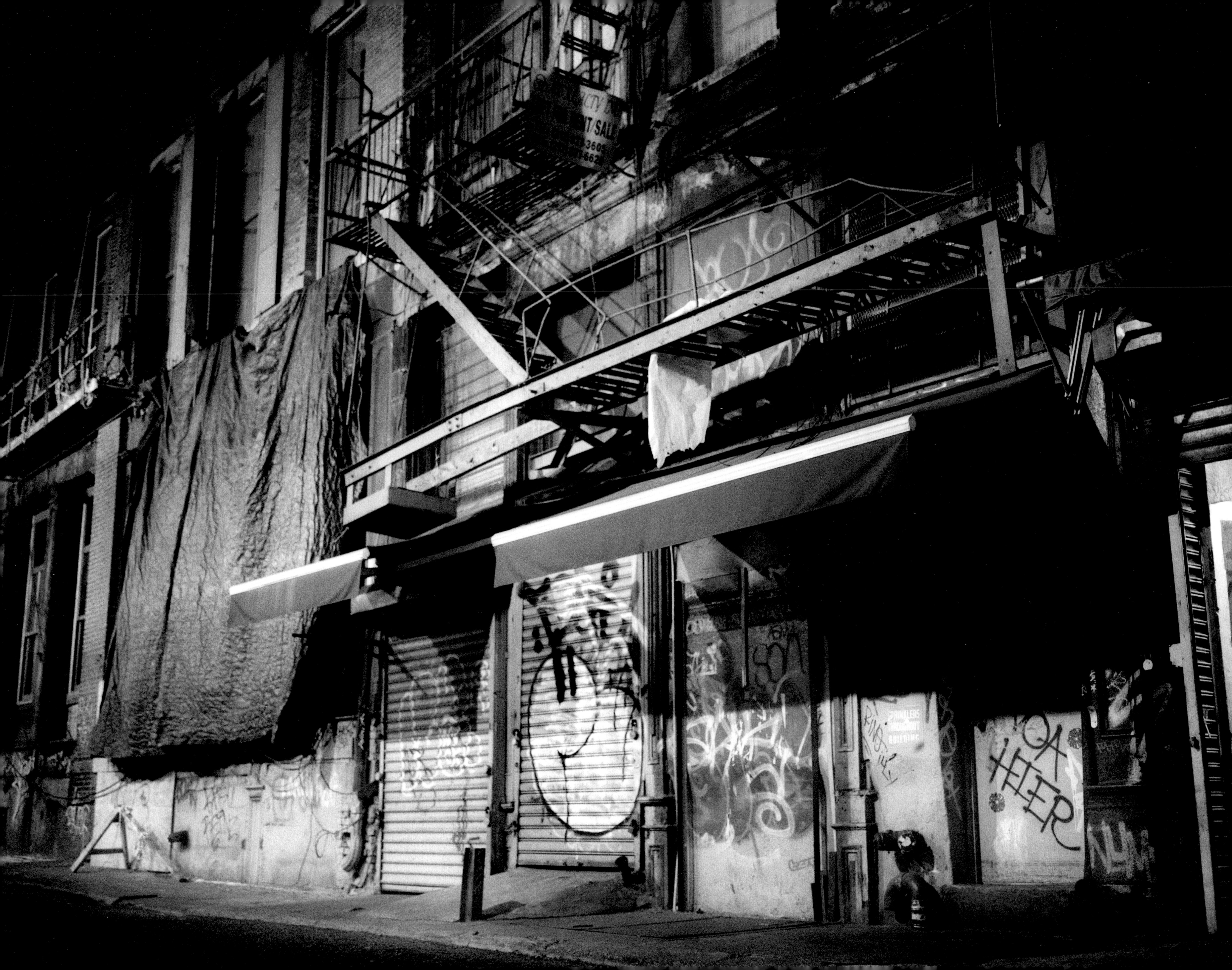

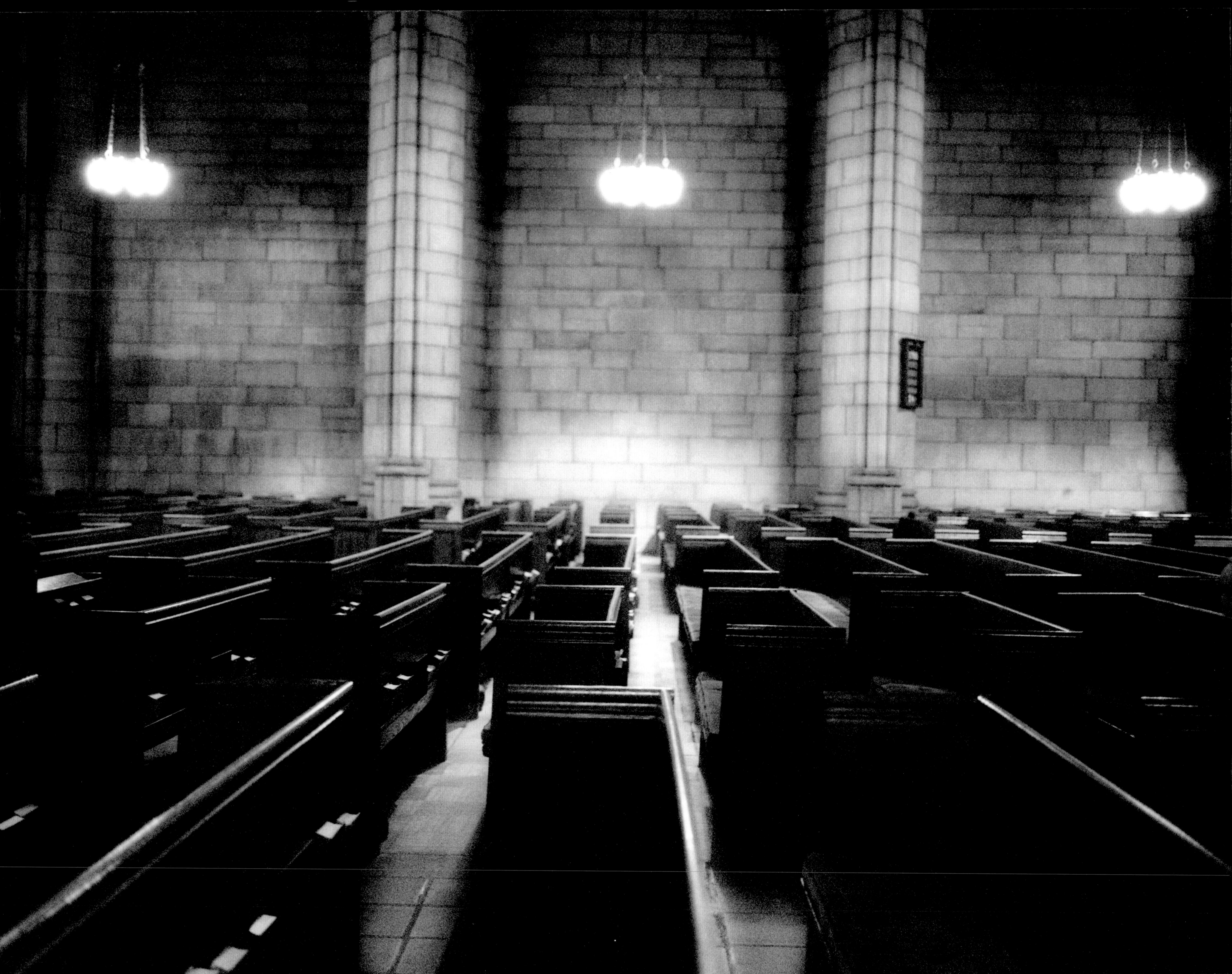

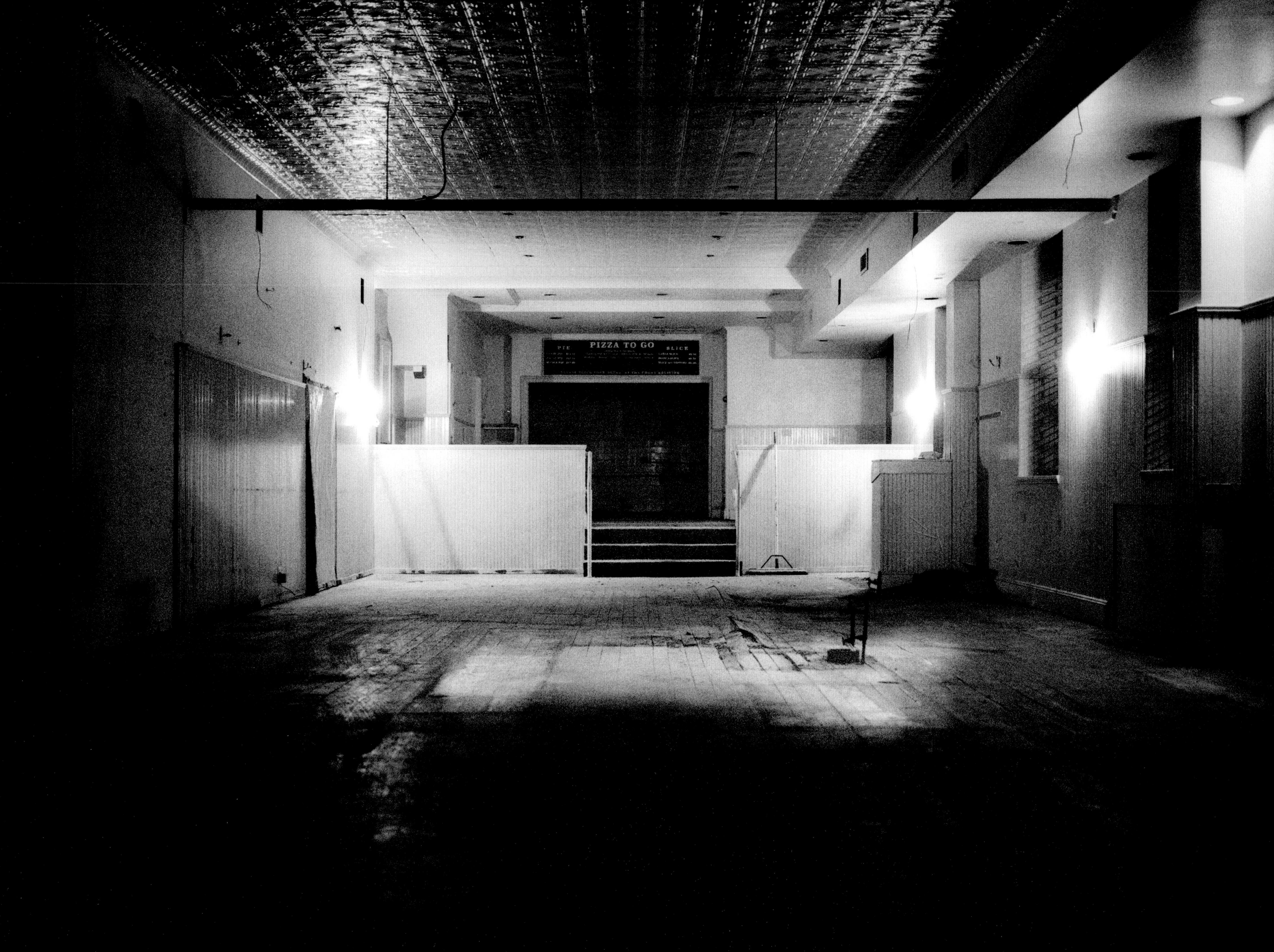
PIE
PIZZA TO GO
SLICE

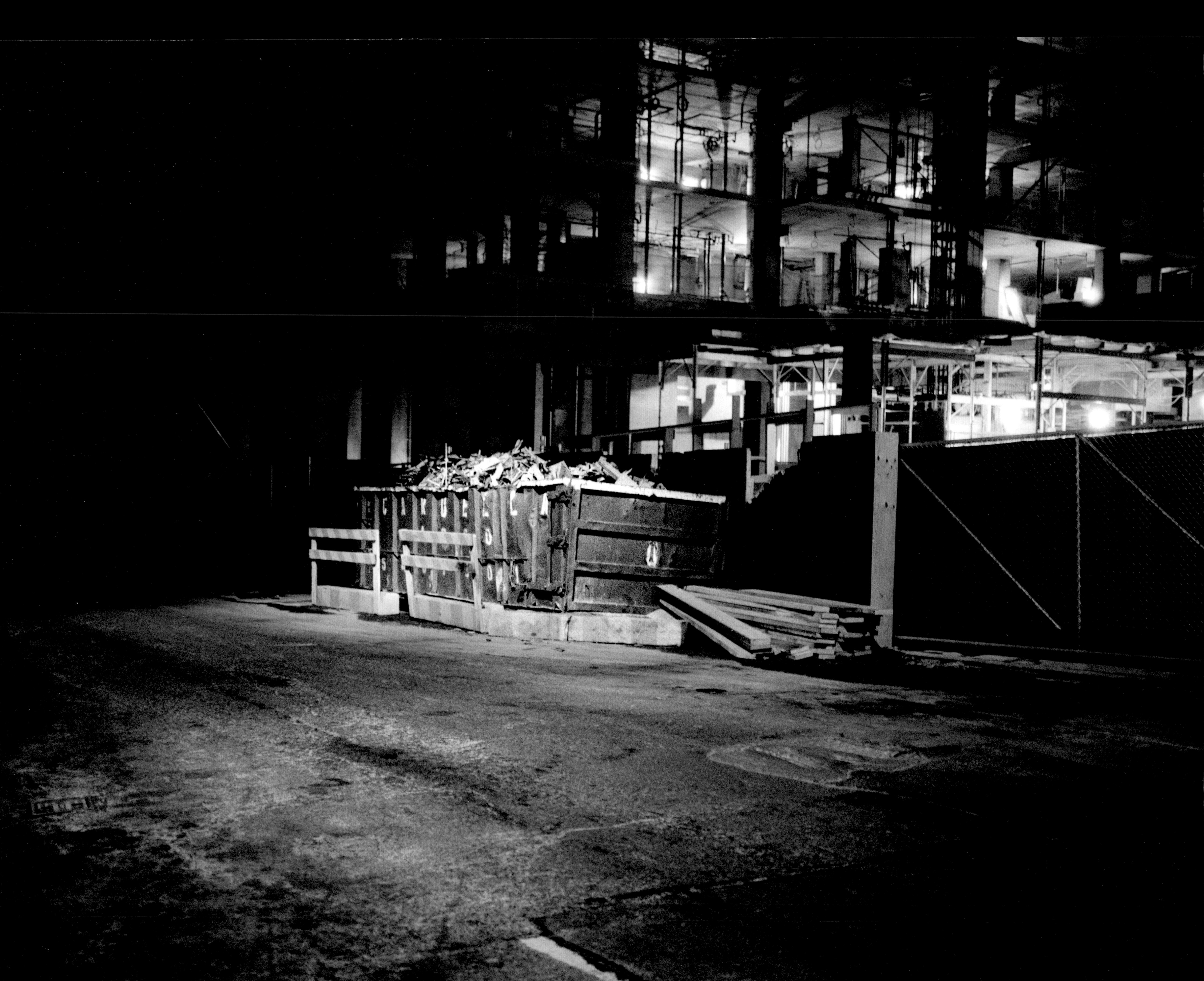

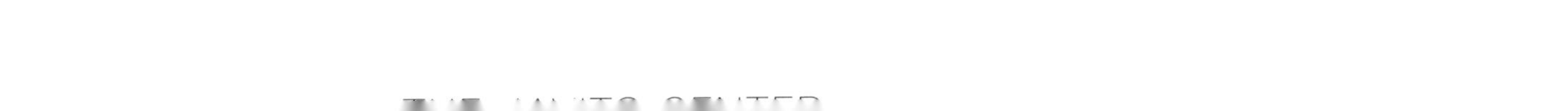

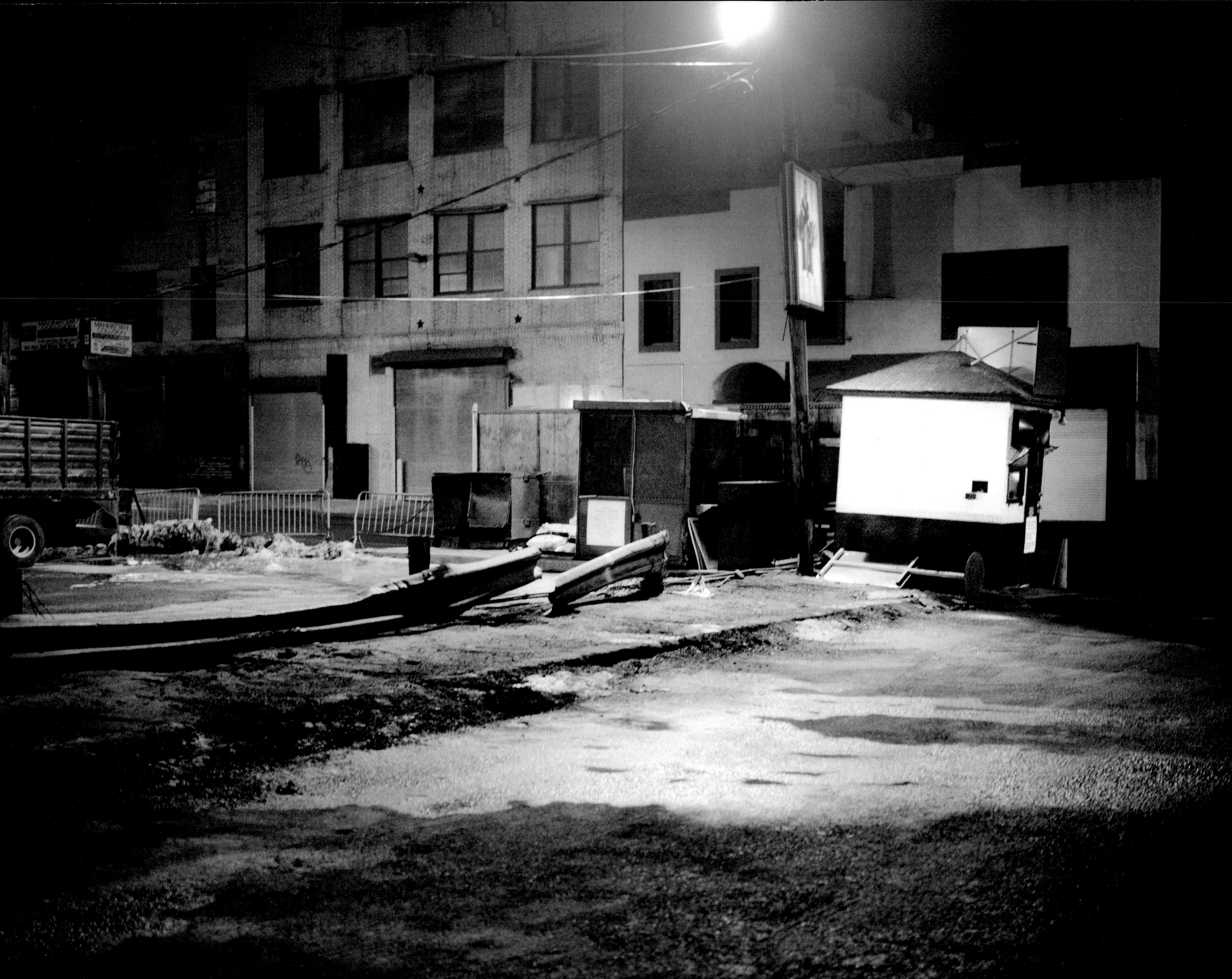

UPPER EAST SIDE

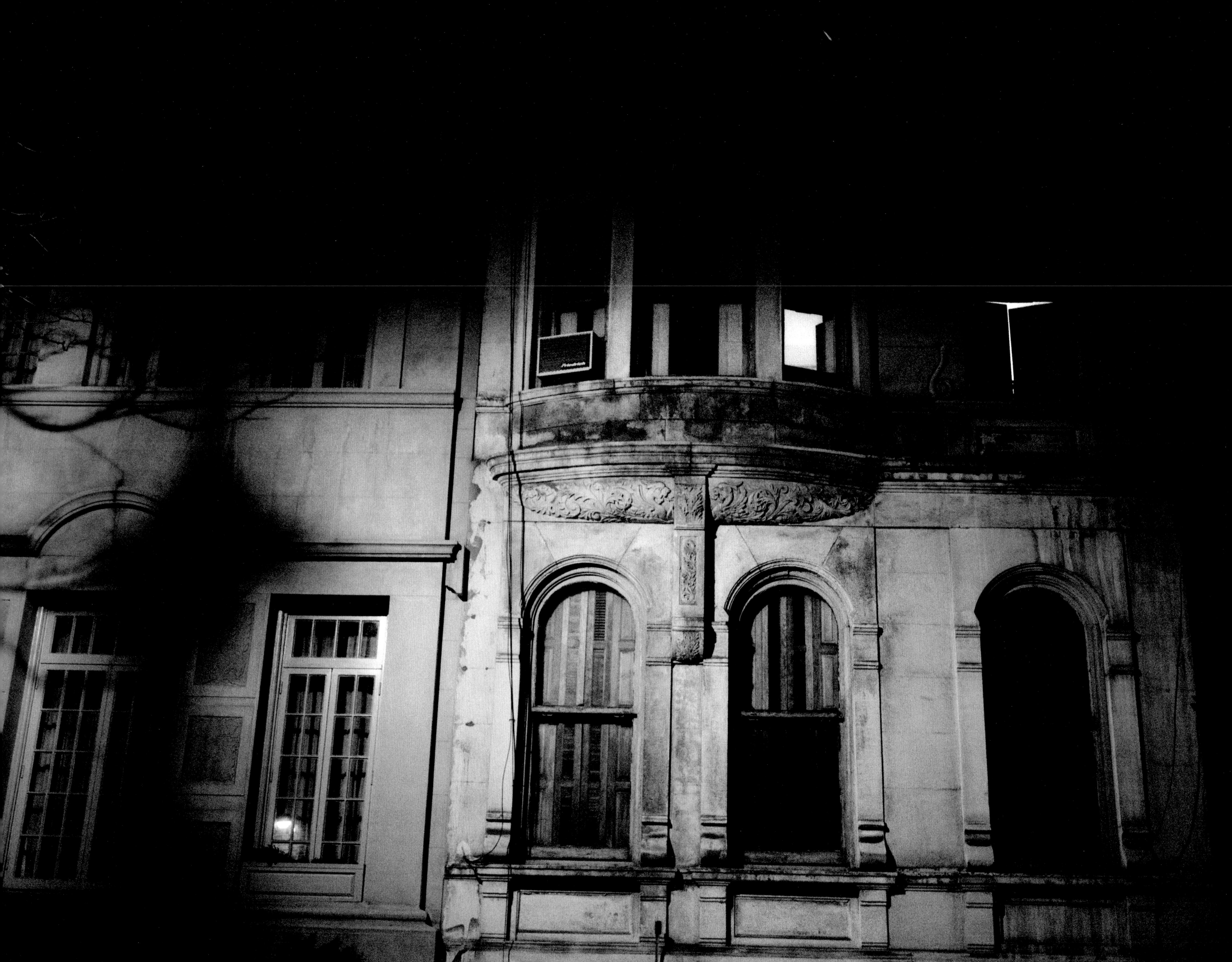

BAY
#15
BAY
#16
CAUTION
BACK IN
OR PULL
OUT ON
GREEN
LIGHT
ONLY

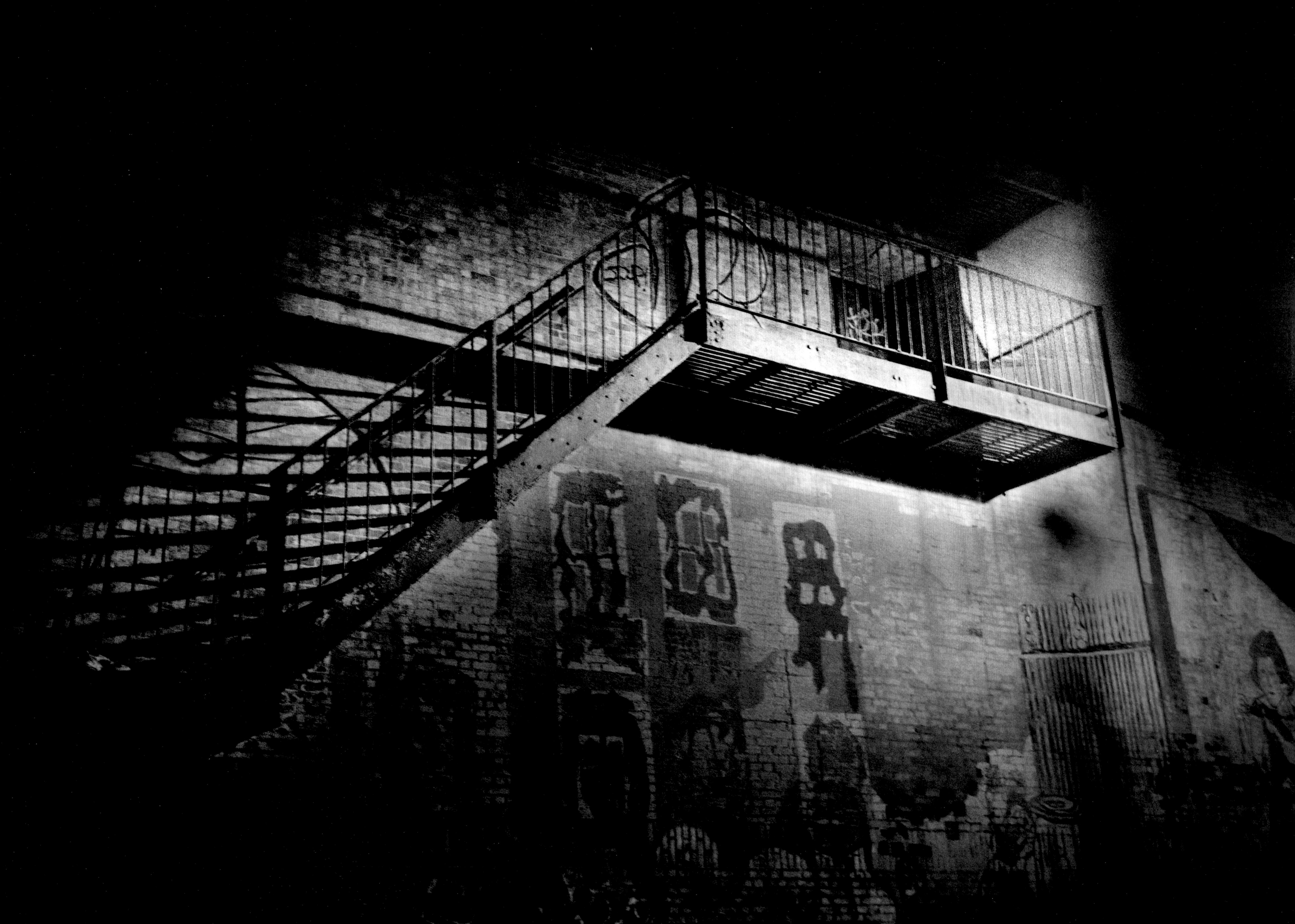

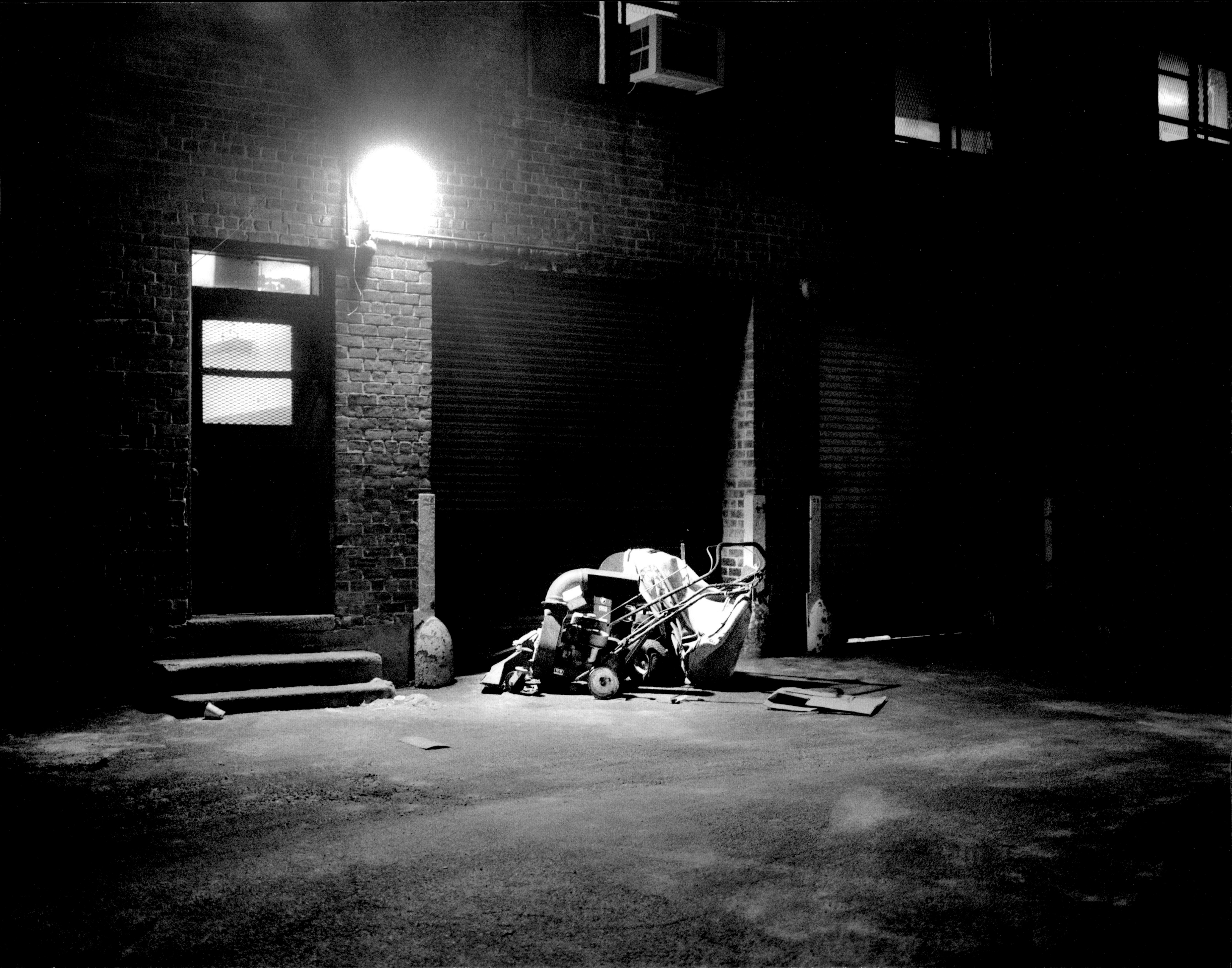

CENTRAL PARK

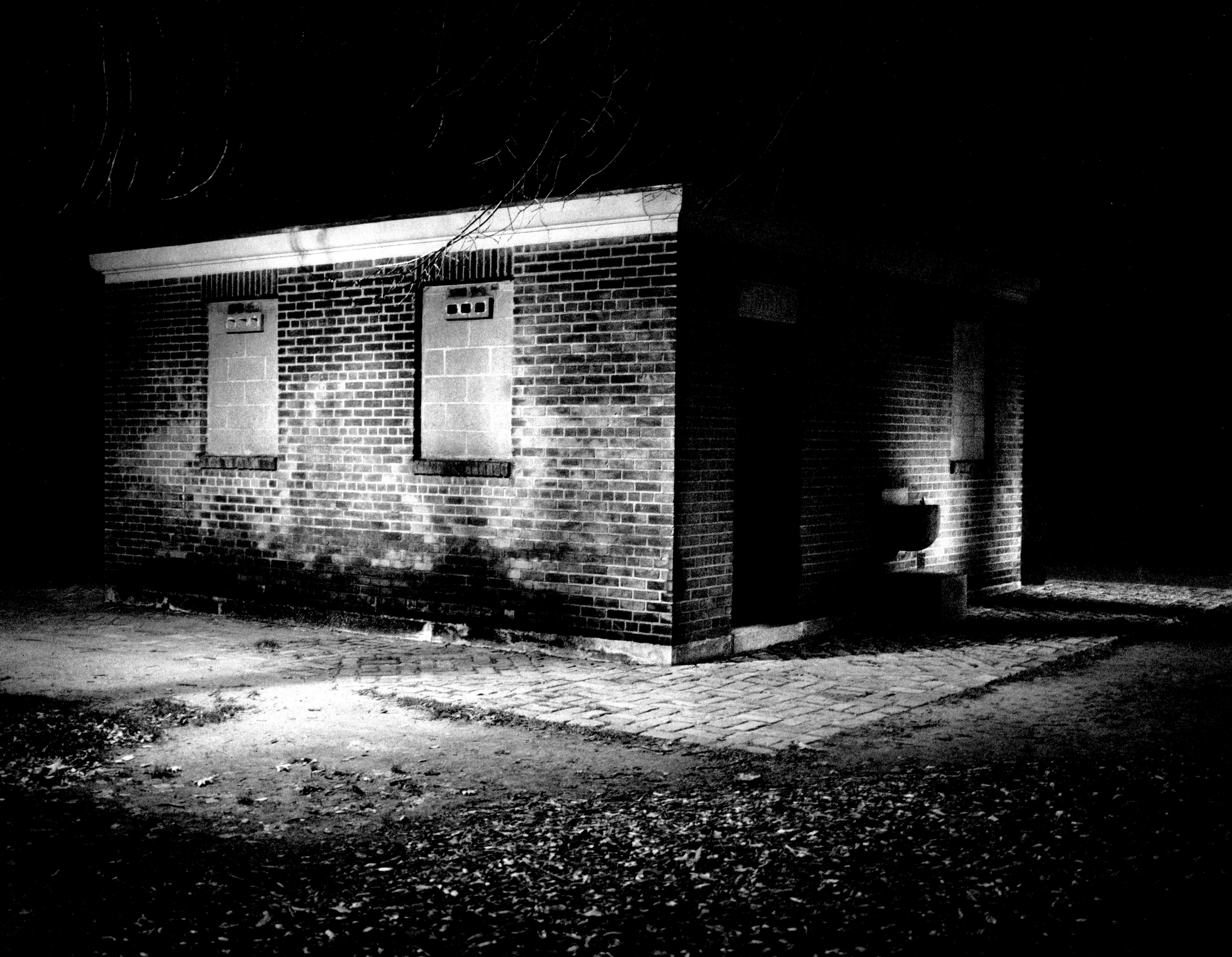

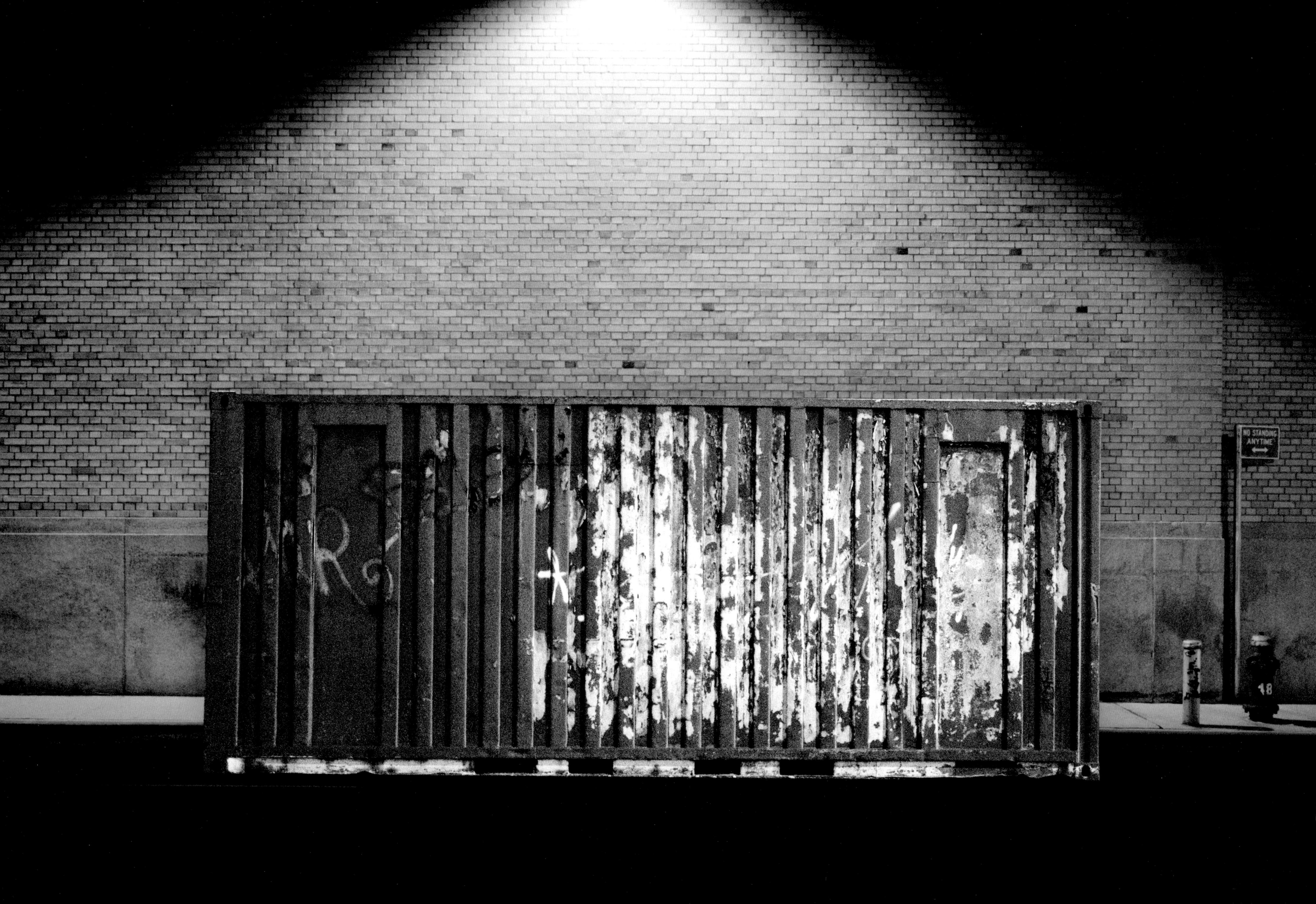
NO STANDING
ANYTIME
18

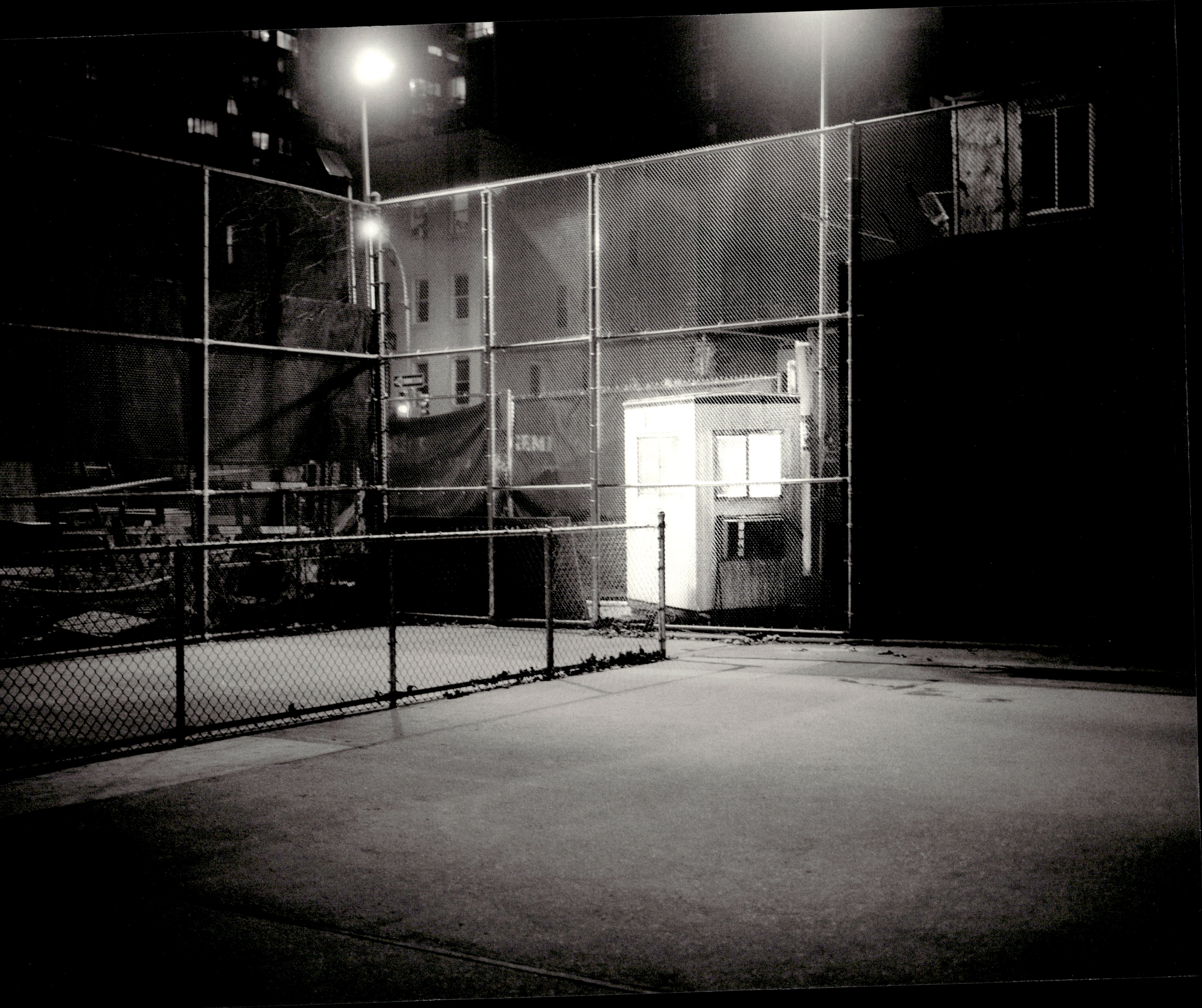

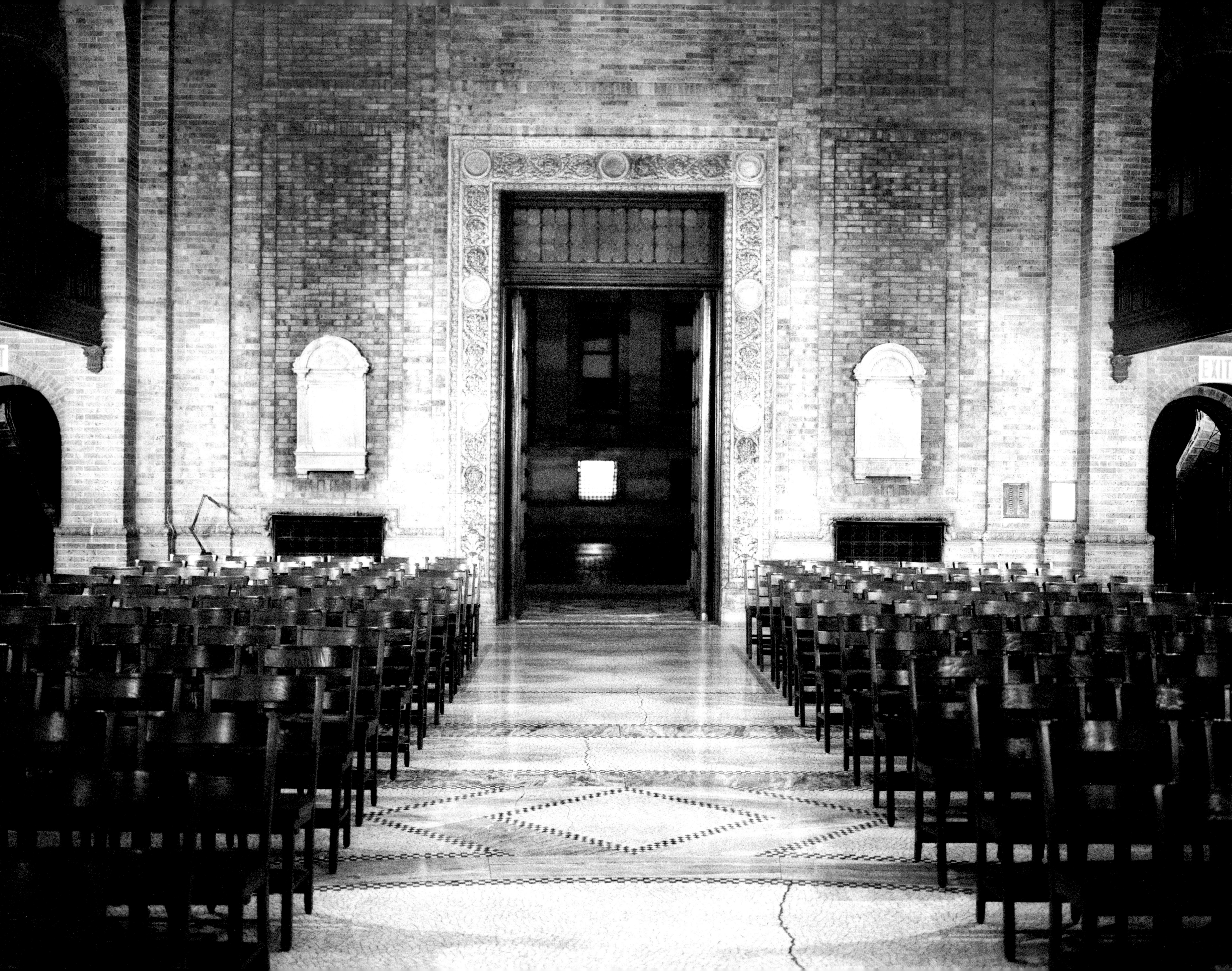
EXIT

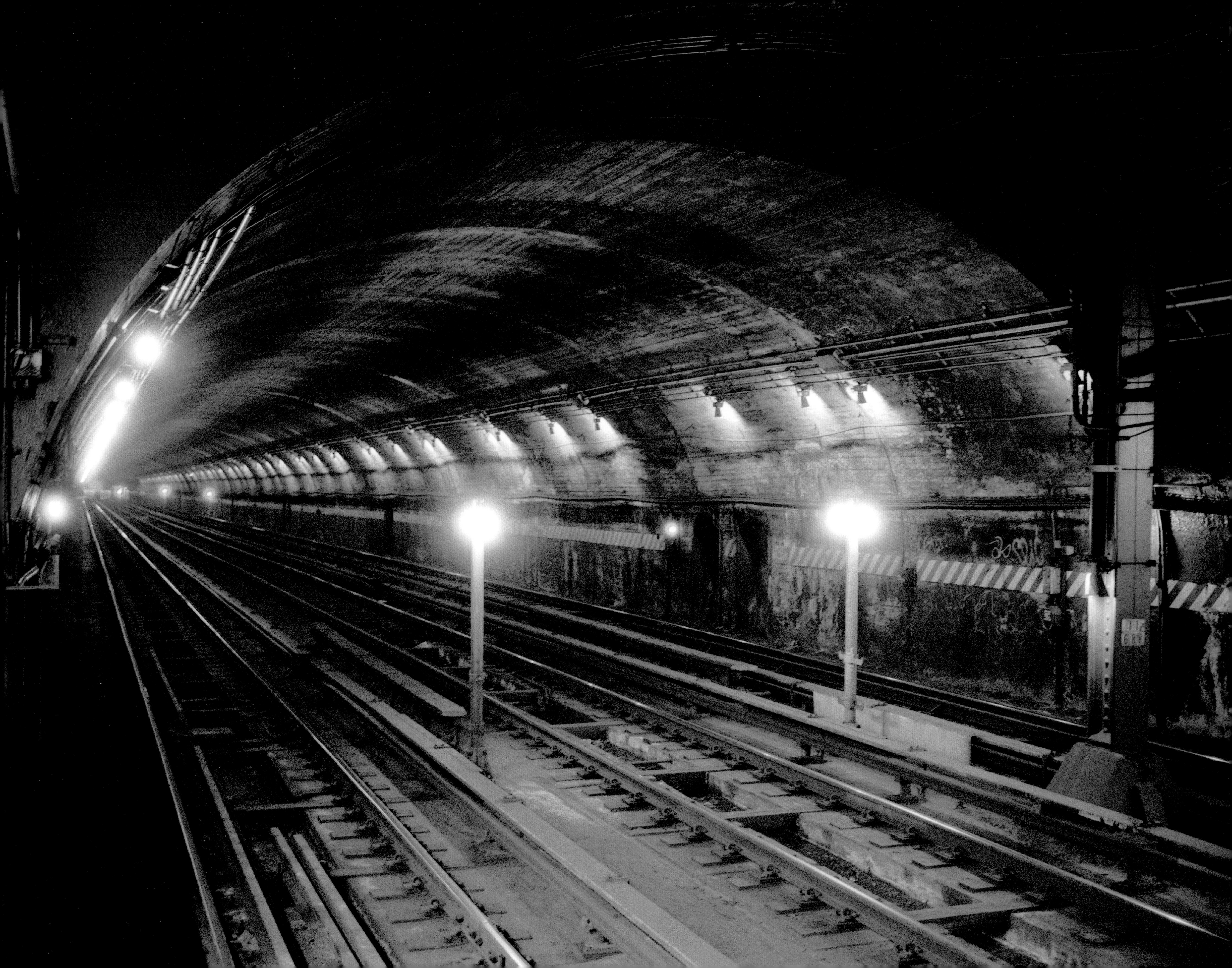

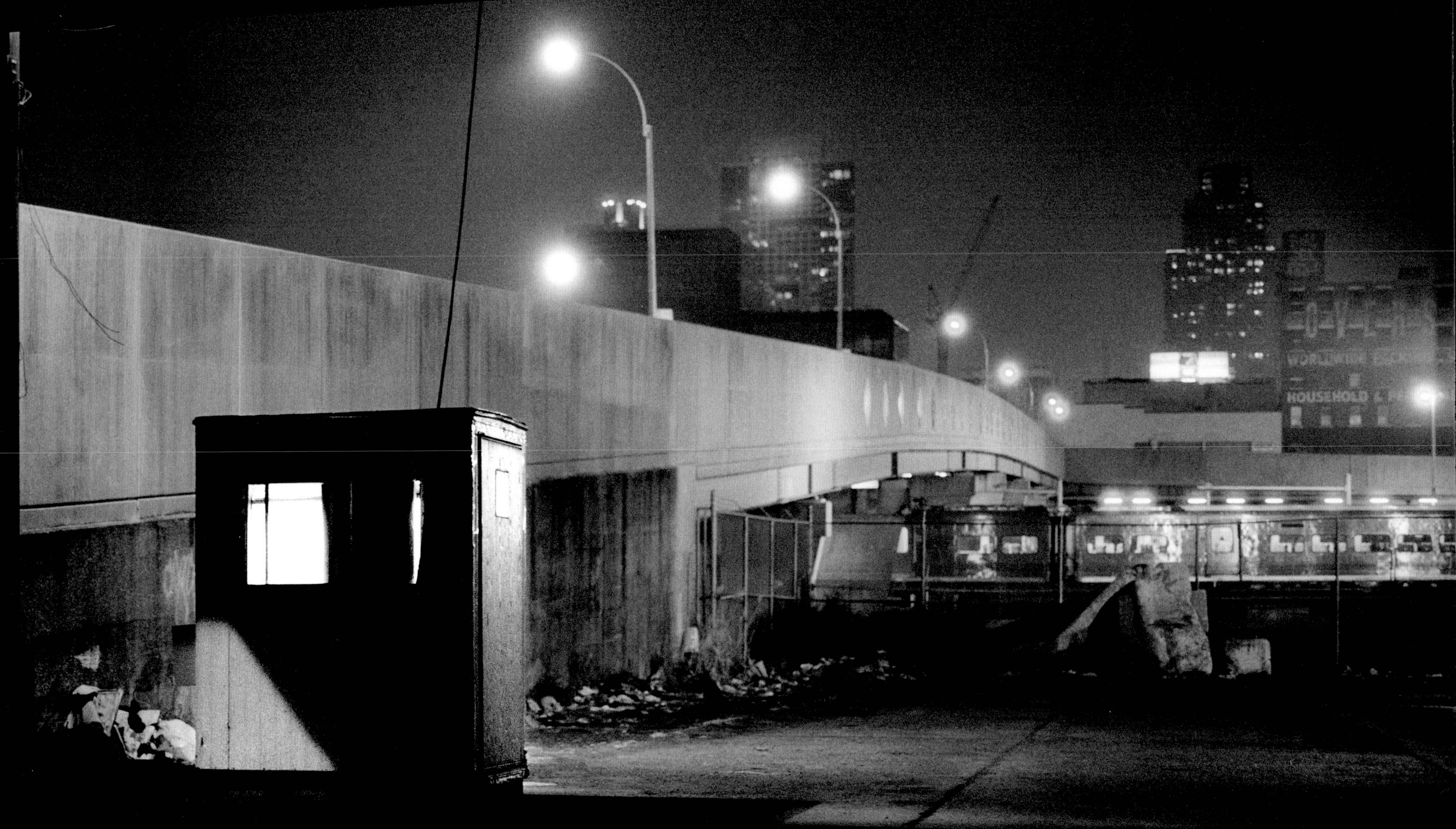
HOUSEHOLD &

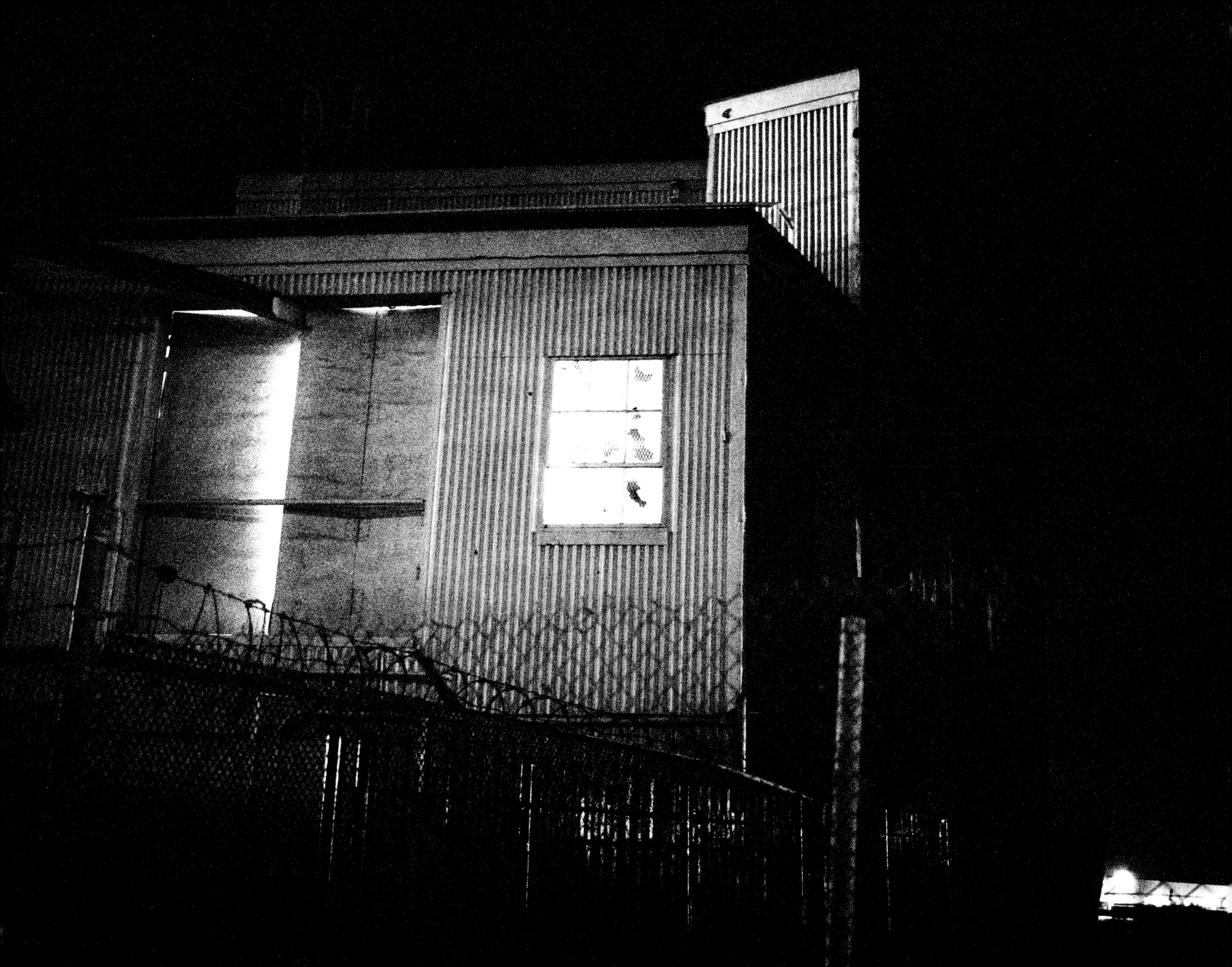

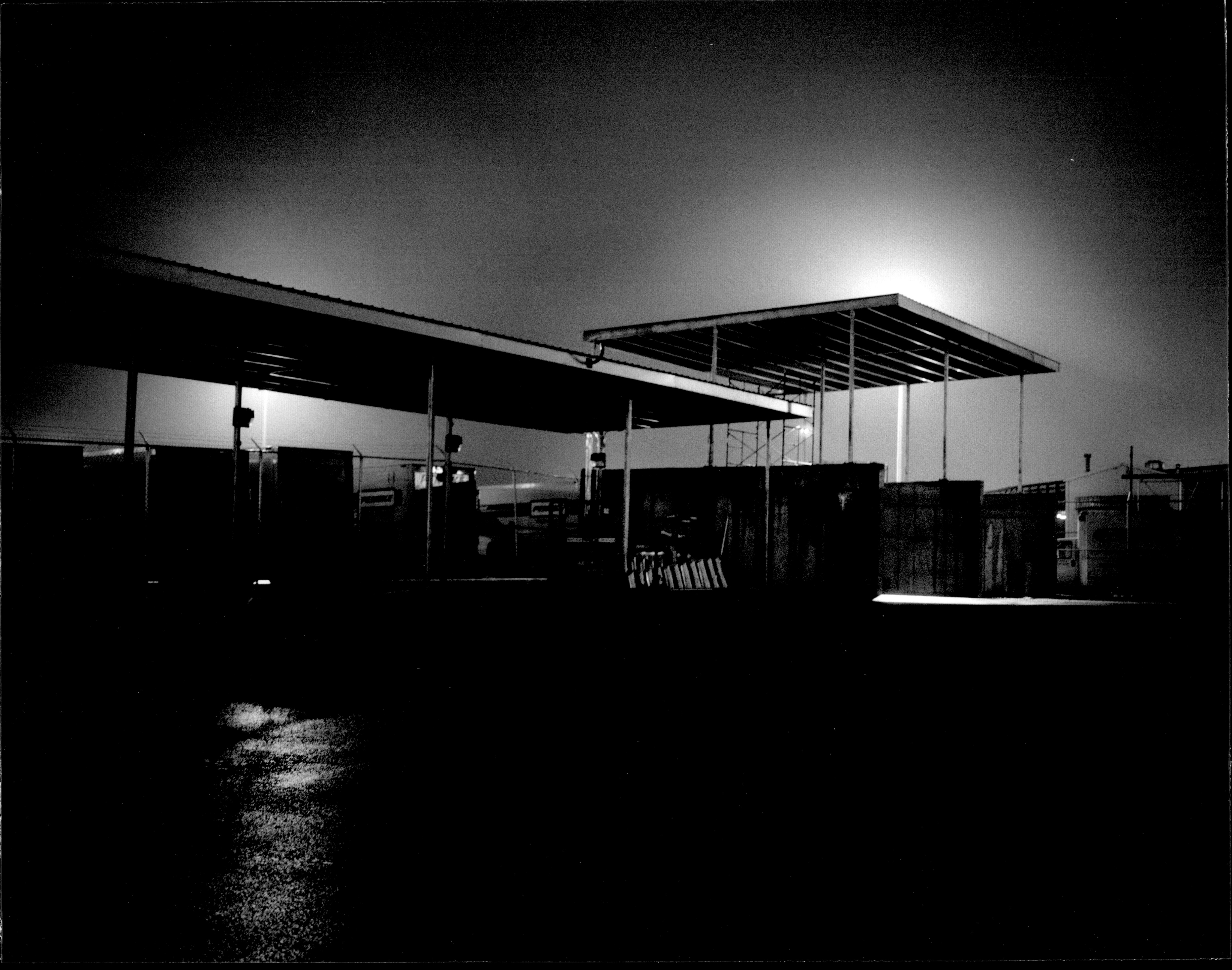

I would like to thank:

Robert Frank who has blessed me with friendship and honored me with his words.

Dodo Jin Ming who has shared her ability to see into other worlds.

Ray Merritt who has been one of my strongest champions and is always there for me.

Joe Cohen who was one of my earliest collectors and supporters.

Ralph Gibson who taught me to look at every square inch.